REMARKABLE
PEOPLE

Shaun White

by Blaine Wiseman

MEDIA ENHANCED BOOKS
AV²
BY WEIGL
ADDED VALUE · AUDIO VISUAL

BOOK CODE

P228351

AV² by Weigl brings you media enhanced books that support active learning.

AV² provides enriched content that supplements and complements this book. Weigl's AV² books strive to create inspired learning and engage young minds for a total learning experience.

Go to **www.av2books.com**, and enter this book's unique code. You will have access to video, audio, web links, quizzes, a slide show, and activities.

Audio
Listen to sections of the book read aloud.

Video
Watch informative video clips.

Web Link
Find research sites and play interactive games.

Try This!
Complete activities and hands-on experiments.

Due to the dynamic nature of the Internet, some of the URLs and activities provided as part of AV² by Weigl may have changed or ceased to exist. AV² by Weigl accepts no responsibility for any such changes. All media enhanced books are regularly monitored to update addresses and sites in a timely manner. Contact AV² by Weigl at 1-866-649-3445 or av2books@weigl.com with any questions, comments, or feedback.

Published by AV² by Weigl
350 5th Avenue, 59th Floor
New York, NY 10118

www.av2books.com   www.weigl.com

Library of Congress Cataloging-in-Publication Data available upon request.
Fax 1-866-44-WEIGL for the attention of the Publishing Records department.

ISBN 978-1-60596-997-8 (hardcover)
ISBN 978-1-60596-998-5 (softcover)

Printed in the United States of America in North Mankato, Minnesota
1 2 3 4 5 6 7 8 9 0 14 13 12 11 10

052010
WEP264000

Editor: Heather C. Hudak
Design: Terry Paulhus

Photograph Credits
Weigl acknowledges Getty Images as the primary image supplier for this title.

Every reasonable effort has been made to trace ownership and to obtain permission to reprint copyright material. The publishers would be pleased to have any errors or omissions brought to their attention so that they may be corrected in subsequent printings.

Contents

Who Is Shaun White?

Shaun White is a **professional** snowboarder and skateboarder. He has won many awards in both sports and is considered one of the greatest extreme athletes in the world. Shaun first began snowboarding when he was six years old. He had his first **sponsorship** one year later. By 13 years of age, Shaun was snowboarding professionally. While snowboarding was his winter passion, Shaun spent the summer months improving his skills as a skateboarder. He became a professional skateboarder when he was 17, and in 2003, Shaun became the first athlete to win medals in both the Winter and Summer **X Games**. Shaun's success on both snow and pavement has led to success in business. This talented athlete has clothing lines, video games, and snowboarding gear designed by and named after him.

"The way I started was I just kept going for one reason, which was I loved the sport."

Growing Up

Shaun Roger White was born in San Diego, California on September 3, 1986. Shaun's father, Roger, worked for the city of San Clemente, California. His mother, Cathy, was a waitress. On weekends, Shaun, along with his sister Kari and brother Jesse, would travel with his parents in the family's van to ski resorts. Later, the family bought a bigger van that they could sleep inside. All five members of the family would sleep in the same motel room.

Shaun was named after his father's favorite athlete, South African surfer Shaun Tomson. Roger wanted his Shaun to become a surfer, and they surfed together often. When Shaun was seven years old, huge waves dragged him underwater while surfing. When he came to the surface for air, Shaun was hit in the face by his surfboard. It was then Shaun decided that he preferred land-based board sports.

■ Like many surfers, Shaun enjoys riding waves on the beaches of Bali, Indonesia.

Get to Know California

ANIMAL
Grizzly Bear

FLAG

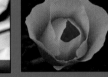
FLOWER
Golden Poppy

California is the birthplace of skateboarding.

California is the most populated state, with more than 36 million people.

In 2003, actor Arnold Schwarzenegger became the governor of California.

Death Valley, California is one of the hottest places on Earth. Temperatures often are higher than 120 degrees Fahrenheit (49 degrees Celsius).

California redwoods are the world's tallest trees. They grow more than 370 feet (113 meters).

Think about it!

Shaun grew up snowboarding, skateboarding, and surfing. He has made a career out of two of these sports. Think of your favorite activities. Could you make a career out of any of these activities?

Practice Makes Perfect

When Shaun was young, his family preferred skiing to snowboarding. On skis, Shaun would go downhill at high speeds. This worried his mother, who encouraged Shaun to try snowboarding. She thought snowboarding would be a safer sport and that Shaun would not be able to travel as quickly.

With the help of his older brother, Shaun became a good snowboarder. By age seven, Shaun had entered his first snowboarding competition. He won the event and earned a chance to compete in the national championships. Shaun's mother sent a video of her son snowboarding to Burton Snowboards. She hoped to impress the company with Shaun's skills. Her plan worked, and Burton decided to sponsor Shaun. The company gave Shaun a new kids' snowboard that they had just developed. Burton remains one of Shaun's sponsors today.

■ Shaun competed in the Burton U.S. Open 2007 Snowboarding Championship.

While working on his snowboarding skills, Shaun also practiced skateboarding. At age nine, Shaun met skateboarding legend Tony Hawk at a local **skate park**. Tony was impressed by the athlete and offered to help Shaun become a professional skater. Shaun met many well-known skateboarders through his friendship with Tony. He was also able to sharpen his skills at Tony's private, indoor skate park.

In 2009, two of Shaun's sponsors, Red Bull and Oakley, teamed up to build a **halfpipe** at Silverton Mountain in Colorado. The pipe, known as Project X, is on the backside of the mountain. It can only be reached by helicopter or snowmobile. At the end of the pipe, there is a large pit filled with foam blocks. Shaun uses Project X to develop new tricks. He showcased one of these tricks during the 2010 Winter Olympics. It is called the **Double McTwist 1260**, also known as the Tomahawk.

Tony Hawk has won more than 70 skateboarding contests in his professional skateboarding career.

Key Events

In 2002, Shaun competed in his very first X Games. At only 15 years of age, Shaun was competing at the world's best-known extreme sports event. Shaun won two medals in the **slopestyle** and halfpipe events at Buttermilk Mountain in Colorado. The next year, he won two gold medals at the X Games.

Four years later, Shaun won his first Summer X Games gold medal for skateboarding. In 2006, he finished eighth place in the **vert** event. The next year, Shaun dramatically improved his skateboarding skills. He became the first person to win gold medals in both the Summer and Winter X Games.

Although Shaun was a well-known athlete in the extreme sports world, he was still unknown to most other sports fans. This changed when he made the 2006 U.S. Olympic team. After winning the Olympic halfpipe gold medal, Shaun became a major celebrity and a hero to millions of fans.

■ Shaun has 16 X Games medals in skateboarding and snowboarding events.

Thoughts from Shaun

Shaun is a role model to millions of people around the world. He is an inspiration to athletes who hope to become professional snowboarders and skateboarders.

Shaun talks about learning to snowboard from his brother Jesse.

"I'd just ride with my bro and get better and better. He's the best guy to be with. I learn so much."

Shaun is very competitive.

"It's what's gotten me so far. It's the worst and best thing about me."

Shaun talks about his home near the ocean.

"In the afternoon, the sun sets in those trees. The beach is right there. It's super awesome."

When he has free time, Shaun enjoys playing guitar.

"I'm awful, but I love playing so much. I'd love to start a band, but I don't have the time for it."

Due to Shaun's success, many companies want him to advertise their products.

"People from these huge **corporations** come to me and ask, 'How can we make this cool?'"

Shaun shares his thoughts about competing in two sports.

"In the winter, I look forward to skating and, in the summer, I look forward to snowboarding. It is a cycle that keeps it fresh."

What Is an Extreme Athlete?

An extreme athlete is someone who practices or competes in extreme sports. Extreme sports are fast-paced, highflying, and often dangerous activities. These sports may include snowboarding, skateboarding, and surfing. Other extreme sports include moto X, snowmobiling, BMX, rally car racing, and wakeboarding. Many of these sports are included in major extreme sports competitions, such as the X Games. Snowboarding is included in the X Games and Winter Olympics.

Snowboarding and skateboarding are the two most popular extreme sports. Snowboarders race down a snow-covered hill performing tricks and stunts. They fly through the air, strapped to a board, twisting and flipping in order to earn points. Skateboarding is similar to snowboarding. A skateboard, however, is much smaller than a snowboard and has wheels on the bottom. Skateboarding events can take place in a halfpipe or on flat land. Skaters push themselves forward with one foot, while balancing on the board with the other foot.

■ The Nokia Air & Style Games are one of many events that showcase snowboarding talent.

Skaters and Snowboarders 101

Tony Hawk (1968–)

After turning professional at 14 years old, Tony later became the most successful skateboarder in history. He began his career with the Dogtown skateboarding team in California. With the help of his teammates, he was the best skateboarder in the world by age 16. In 103 professional competitions, Tony finished in first place 73 times and second place 19 times. During the 1999 X Games, Tony became the first skateboarder to complete a **900**.

Elissa Steamer (1975–)

One of the greatest female skaters in history, Elissa is well known for her street skateboarding skills. Elissa was one of the first female stars of the sport and the first female character in a skateboarding video game. In 1998, she won her first major event, the Slam City Jam. She repeated her win the following year. In 2004, Elissa won her first X Games gold medal in the Street event. It was her first of three straight X Games gold medals. In 2008, Elissa won her fourth gold medal at the X Games.

Terje Haakonsen (1974–)

Terje Haakonsen is considered one of the greatest snowboarders in history. The Norwegian star has won many events around the world in halfpipe competition and is one of the most influential **back country** riders. Born in Norway, Terje loves to explore mountains for the good **terrain**. There is even a trick named after him. In the Haakon flip, riders take off backward and perform a somersault and two full spins in the air before landing forward.

Hannah Teter (1987–)

Hannah started snowboarding when she was eight years old. She learned the sport from her two older brothers, who were professional snowboarders. Living in Vermont, Hannah trained on the nearby mountains in winter. During summer, she would practice her high-flying moves on a trampoline. In 2006, Hannah won the Olympic halfpipe gold medal. She uses all of the money she wins during competitions to help the less fortunate and people suffering from **AIDS** in Kenya.

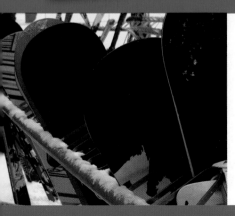

Board Sports

Snowboarding and skateboarding are fairly new sports, but board sports date back hundreds of years. Surfing is the original board sport. People in **Polynesia** used wooden boards to surf on top of ocean waves as early as the 16th century. Snowboarding and skateboarding are both based on surfing. The skateboard was invented by a surfer, who used the board to get to the beach. The sport was originally called sidewalk surfing. The very first snowboard was called a snurfer, which comes from the words "snow" and "surf."

Influences

Although Shaun does not compete in team sports, he knows that many people have helped him achieve success. His biggest influence has been his older brother, Jesse. When Shaun first started snowboarding, he would follow Jesse down mountains, copying his brother's moves. Jesse would challenge Shaun, telling him to try certain tricks. Being challenged by his brother helped Shaun push himself to try more difficult stunts and improve his skills.

Another influence in Shaun's life is Tony Hawk. Tony dominated the skateboarding world for two decades. Tony saw Shaun's talent and knew that he could help the young skater become a great athlete. Shaun learned from Tony by watching the way Tony handled the pressure of being a top athlete.

■ Cathy White is a strong supporter of her son Shaun's career. She displayed a bag with Shaun's picture at the snowboard halfpipe medal ceremony in Vancouver.

Often, people would ask Tony for pictures and autographs. Watching his **mentor**, Shaun learned how to handle this kind of attention. Tony also gave Shaun business advice about which companies he should **endorse**. Shaun learned from his friend's example. Like Tony, Shaun has become one of the most successful extreme athletes in the world, both on the board and in business.

THE WHITE FAMILY

Family is very important to Shaun. His parents and siblings have helped him in many areas, including school, sports, and business. The family's weekend trips to the mountains helped Shaun develop his skills. Support from his parents helped him become a professional athlete. When Shaun earned enough money to buy his own house, his parents and sister moved in with him. Shaun's brother lives down the street from the rest of the family. Jesse helps Shaun design his clothing and make other business decisions.

■ The entire White family now snowboards. Jesse designs for Burton Snowboards. Kari won the 2000 U.S. Open Junior Halfpipe Championship.

Overcoming Obstacles

It takes determination to become a great athlete, and Shaun has faced many obstacles on his path to success. Shaun was born with a serious heart condition. It can cause severe lung problems and make exercise difficult. Before he was one year old, Shaun had two heart surgeries. The surgeries left Shaun with a scar on his chest, but his heart began to work properly. Sometimes, when Shaun gets excited, his scar tingles.

Another obstacle that Shaun has faced throughout his career is the danger of performing extreme sports moves. When athletes fly through the air at high speeds, performing extreme stunts, accidents and injuries happen.

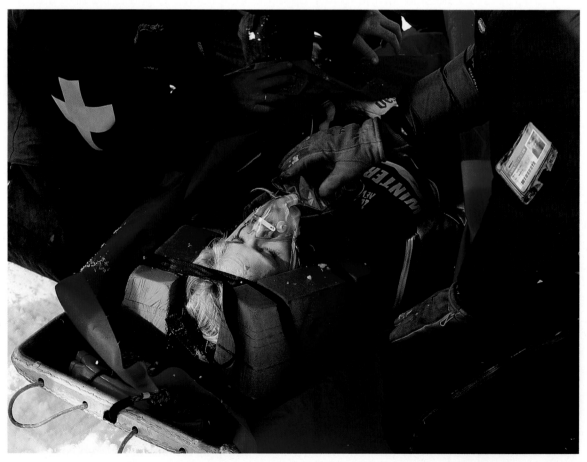

■ Snowboarder Britte Van der Pouw was assisted by medical staff after a fall in 2009.

At 11 years of age, Shaun was skateboarding in an event for MTV. He was performing a trick when he crashed mid-air into another skater, Bob Burnquist. Burnquist was much older and bigger than Shaun. The crash broke Shaun's foot and arm and cracked his skull.

In 2004, Shaun injured his knee competing at the X Games. He needed surgery to repair the knee. After the surgery, Shaun was unable to use his leg for several months. Being inactive made his leg muscles shrink. Once Shaun's knee healed, Shaun spent time in the gym every day so that he could exercise his leg muscles.

■ Bob Burnquist's peers have voted him "best vert skateboarder" three times.

Achievements and Successes

In total, Shaun has won 10 gold medals in snowboarding at the Winter X Games and a gold at the Summer X Games in skateboarding. Being a top athlete in both sports has helped Shaun build his reputation as one of the greatest athletes in the world.

Shaun's greatest achievements as a snowboarder have come at the Winter Olympics. In 2006, he set a halfpipe record by earning the highest score in history. He also won the gold medal at the event. At the 2010 Winter Olympics, Shaun set a new record. He scored so high on his first run that he knew he had won gold before any of the other snowboarders made a second run.

■ Shaun White's successes in snowboarding have made him a celebrity. In 2010, Shaun was a presenter at Nickelodeon's Kids' Choice Awards.

Shaun did not have to take a second run at the event. However, he decided to perform some dangerous new moves for the crowd. It did not matter if he fell, Shaun had already won gold. Shaun broke his own record from the previous Olympics and won his second Olympic gold medal.

Many companies want Shaun to help sell their products. Shaun earns about $9 million each year from his sponsors. He gets money from companies such as Mountain Dew and Target. By making smart business decisions, Shaun has ensured that he will remain a popular spokesperson for many years.

TARGET HOUSE

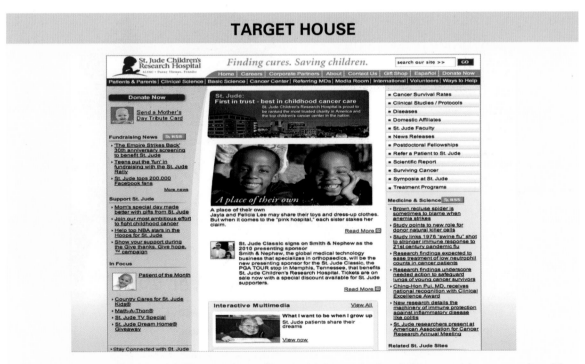

Shaun's partnership with Target has allowed him to help children with severe health problems. Located in Memphis, Target House is a place where sick children and their families can live while the children receive treatment for their illness. Shaun often visits Target House to talk with children and help them through their illness. He designed and built the Shaun White Great Room where children can spend time together and make new friends. For more information on Target House, visit **www.stjude.org**.

Write a Biography

A person's life story can be the subject of a book. This kind of book is called a biography. Biographies describe the lives of remarkable people, such as those who have achieved great success or have done important things to help others. These people may be alive today, or they may have lived many years ago. Reading a biography can help you learn more about a remarkable person.

At school, you might be asked to write a biography. First, decide whom you want to write about. You can choose an extreme athlete, such as Shaun White, or any other person you find interesting. Then, find out if your library has any books about this person.

Learn as much as you can about him or her. Write down the key events in the person's life. What was this person's childhood like? What has he or she accomplished? What are his or her goals? What makes this person special or unusual?

A concept web is a useful research tool. Read the questions in the following concept web. Answer the questions in your notebook. Your answers will help you write your biography.

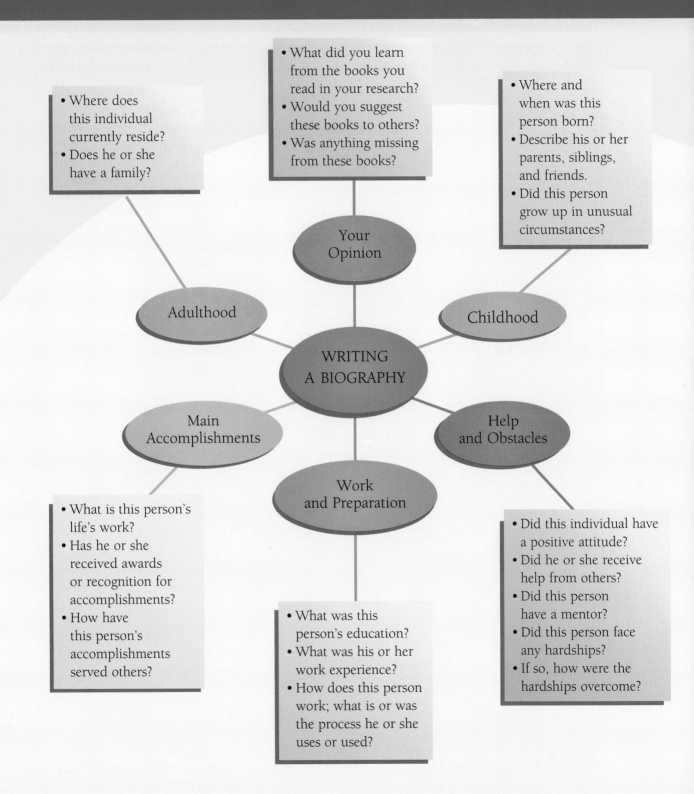

- What did you learn from the books you read in your research?
- Would you suggest these books to others?
- Was anything missing from these books?

- Where does this individual currently reside?
- Does he or she have a family?

- Where and when was this person born?
- Describe his or her parents, siblings, and friends.
- Did this person grow up in unusual circumstances?

Your Opinion

Adulthood

Childhood

WRITING A BIOGRAPHY

Main Accomplishments

Help and Obstacles

Work and Preparation

- What is this person's life's work?
- Has he or she received awards or recognition for accomplishments?
- How have this person's accomplishments served others?

- What was this person's education?
- What was his or her work experience?
- How does this person work; what is or was the process he or she uses or used?

- Did this individual have a positive attitude?
- Did he or she receive help from others?
- Did this person have a mentor?
- Did this person face any hardships?
- If so, how were the hardships overcome?

Timeline

YEAR	SHAUN WHITE	WORLD EVENTS
1986	Shaun is born on September 3.	Michael Jordan scores 63 points in one game to set an NBA playoff record.
1992	Shaun begins snowboarding.	The Winter Olympics are held in Albertville, France. The Summer Olympics take place in Barcelona, Spain.
1999	Shaun becomes a professional snowboarder.	The United States wins the Women's World Cup of soccer in front of the largest crowd in women's sports history.
2003	Shaun wins his first Winter X Games gold medal.	Lebron James begins his NBA career.
2006	Shaun wins his first Olympic gold medal.	The Pittsburgh Steelers defeat the Seattle Seahawks to win Super Bowl XL.
2007	Shaun wins his first Summer X Games gold medal.	Soccer legend David Beckham joins the Los Angeles Galaxy of Major League Soccer.
2010	Shaun wins his second Olympic gold medal.	American Alpine skier Lindsey Vonn wins gold in the Ladies' Downhill event at the 2010 Vancouver Olympics.

Words to Know

900: a trick that consists of two-and-a-half complete rotations in the air

AIDS: a deadly virus that makes it difficult for the body to fight infections

back country: an underdeveloped area outside cities or towns

corporations: large companies

Double McTwist 1260: a trick that includes two twists and three-and-a-half rotations while flipping in the air.

endorse: to publicly support something

halfpipe: a structure with two long, curved walls, used for performing tricks in skateboarding and snowboarding

mentor: a teacher or coach

Polynesia: a group of islands in the Pacific Ocean

professional: a person who is paid to do an activity

skate park: a skateboarding venue consisting of ramps, rails, and other structures used for performing tricks

slopestyle: a competition that combines speed and style

sponsorship: a company that pays someone or gives them free equipment and products in exchange for advertising

terrain: the features of an area of land

vert: a vertical jump

X Games: an annual extreme sports competition

Index

Log on to www.av2books.com

AV² by Weigl brings you media enhanced books that support active learning. Go to **www.av2books.com**, and enter the special code inside the front cover of this book. You will gain access to enriched and enhanced content that supplements and complements this book. Content includes video, audio, web links, quizzes, a slide show, and activities.

Audio
Listen to sections of the book read aloud.

Video
Watch informative video clips.

Web Link
Find research sites and play interactive games.

Try This!
Complete activities and hands-on experiments.

WHAT'S ONLINE?

Try This! Complete activities and hands-on experiments.	**Web Link** Find research sites and play interactive games.	**Video** Watch informative video clips.	**EXTRA FEATURES**
Pages 6-7 Complete an activity about your childhood.	**Pages 8-9** Learn more about Shaun White's life.	**Pages 4-5** Watch a video about Shaun White.	**Audio** Hear introductory audio at the top of every page.
Pages 10-11 Try this activity about key events.	**Pages 14-15** Find out more about the people who influenced Shaun White.	**Pages 12-13** Check out a video about Shaun White.	**Key Words** Study vocabulary, and play a matching word game.
Pages 16-17 Complete an activity about overcoming obstacles.	**Pages 18-19** Learn more about Shaun White's achievements.		**Slide Show** View images and captions, and try a writing activity.
Pages 20-21 Write a biography.	**Pages 20-21** Check out this site about Shaun White.		**AV² Quiz** Take this quiz to test your knowledge
Page 22 Try this timeline activity.			

Due to the dynamic nature of the Internet, some of the URLs and activities provided as part of AV² by Weigl may have changed or ceased to exist. AV² by Weigl accepts no responsibility for any such changes. All media enhanced books are regularly monitored to update addresses and sites in a timely manner. Contact AV² by Weigl at 1-866-649-3445 or av2books@weigl.com with any questions, comments, or feedback.